Forgotten California

poems by

Bonnie Hearn Hill

Finishing Line Press
Georgetown, Kentucky

Forgotten California

Copyright © 2023 by Bonnie Hearn Hill
ISBN 979-8-88838-288-2 First Edition
All rights reserved under International and Pan-American Copyright Conventions. No part of this book may be reproduced in any manner whatsoever without written permission from the publisher, except in the case of brief quotations embodied in critical articles and reviews.

ACKNOWLEDGMENTS

"Bat, Butterfly, Moth," and "Blackstone Avenue," Pacific Journal, Fresno Pacific University, Fall 2022
"Even These Days," The Journal of Radical Wonder, May 2022
"Judith Shakespeare Goes Postal," and "Window," Ursa Minor, UC Berkeley, 2018

Publisher: Leah Huete de Maines
Editor: Christen Kincaid
Cover Art: *River Bird*, Larry Hill
Author Photo: H. Dixon
Cover Design: Elizabeth Maines McCleavy

Order online: www.finishinglinepress.com
also available on amazon.com

Author inquiries and mail orders:
Finishing Line Press
PO Box 1626
Georgetown, Kentucky 40324
USA

Table of Contents

Outside Tijuana 1

Even These Days 2

On the Town 3

After Ten Years 4

Alfonso Trotter Never Could Write Too Well..................... 5

The Trip Out 6

The Parrot of Easton 8

Blackstone Avenue 9

Judith Shakespeare Goes Postal 10

You Imagine 12

The Way They Leave 14

All The Time 15

Momentary Women 16

Eating the Poems 17

Napa Valley Diptych 18

Sequoia 19

Bat, Butterfly, Moth 20

October Abstract 21

For Larry

Outside Tijuana

There are no women at this wall
of corrugated tin, only dark men
in heavy shirts, watching the water
and the lights beyond.

One carries a stepladder. Another
swallows what is left of the day
from a can of Tecate.

When sunset slips into night,
they will try again.
The ladder will grow.
The men will rise taller in their shoes.
As the border unwinds before them
like a thin ribbon, those behind
will wait at the wall like children,
wishing on stars,
praying to San Diego.

Even These Days

The walnut squirrels
are the size of Pomeranians.
They make their way through
the container garden in the
early morning
when the air quality is
triple digits, even these days
when smoke from the wildfires
covers the San Joaquin Valley.

As they yank the sweet potatoes,
leaving only clumps of black soil
like tiny fists on the redwood,
I watch from the quarantined
kitchen and wonder.
How does a raw sweet potato
taste to an animal whose only
sky is a lid of smoke?

On the Town

Sequoia trees
wear aluminum skirts
covering their legs
and hope their roots hold.
A hot night out.

In the back of the closet,
blue ballet shoes are
almost invisible among
sandals, heels, boots,
and toeless Pilates socks.

Blue satin shoes.
They lie empty now,
their round heels still untested,
their stiff toes still undanced.

After Ten Years

Drunk at the backyard table,
he attempts to impale a fly
with his toothpick because, he says,
flies are no good to anyone.

His grave has grown around him
like a tract of homes. He has not
noticed that he can no longer
stretch his arms without touching
something, that his woman must
turn her back to his face in order to sleep.

He is unable to hear the voice
of the boy no chamber can contain,
his children trying to breathe
beneath their pillows.

After ten years, he is still drinking
the tired gin of return, tormented
only by the buzzing above
his paper plate of rice and chicken.

Alfonso Trotter Never Could Write Too Well

But he fought well enough to make the team
and died, as the faculty predicted, before
his twenty-first year. As the faculty failed
to predict, he died, not in the gas
chamber, but on a blood-gray street
on the south side of Hanford, California,
a sharpened rat-tail comb in his chest.

He was our outlaw because he was
the only one we had. The boys gave
him quarters. The girls ran from his
taunting music, imagining
themselves angry.

Now, he is dead, and no one
is surprised, not even his youngest
brother, whose rigid eyes remind me
of Alfonso Trotter in the first grade,
clutching a blunt pencil in his
wet fingers.

The Trip Out

"Your daddy was always in the wrong place
at the wrong time," my mother will later recall.
Trouble was, he never knew it until he got there."
Today, nobody knows it, we girls lined
like pennies on the seat, new purses and coins
for the train trip to California, Ila using hers
to summon the men with sandwiches and candy,
richer at this moment than she will ever be again.

Nailed to my portion of the bench, I feel my silver
through the corded envelope, saving it for the conductor
with a swelling stomach and starched white shirt
like the men who walked our property those days
before we left. "Where's yours?"
the conductor will ask, and I will hold mine high.

Later, we will claim our names. Ila will be
the one we call fragile, Eva, the runaway,
Vera, the beauty. I will be the worker, with a job
at Mrs. Hamby's store, smelling the fabric I sew
for my sisters at night, organdy flowers floating
in a bowl, the only pastel dreams at those
Riverdale dances, their skirts bobbed like our hair—
how my father will hate me the day I bob our hair,
Vera squealing, "Carrie did it, Daddy. Carrie did it,"
Ila standing silent in a guilty, golden pile.

I will be the one who gets out, who moves
to the hot plate of the city, where supper is eaten
standing up, and the foghorns under the Golden Gate
begin to sound like home.
But today, I am part of the whole,
my cotton-print dress weary as my mother, stooped
across the aisle with the baby.
In the bathroom, we wash up, Ila hypnotized
by the common comb hanging from a chain.
I slap her hand, knowing that if she touches
that comb, we will all be lost forever.

This is where our trip begins, the men carrying their hopes
in their fingers, my mother carrying hers in her lap.
I clutch mine tightly in my purse, the jagged differences
growing between us on the train, already beginning
to divide us like so many parcels of land.

The Parrot of Easton

I imagine the Parrots as a flocked family
of birds on an oak tree in Easton,
the broken arm of Fresno, California,
over a bar named Gladys Hideout, which
the regulars pronounce Gladeez,
like something you might sing in church.

I imagine Wilby Parrot, the Army vet,
in his pastel feathers, his ironed everything,
right down to his socks.

He is so full of memory, Wilby,
that every day when it is time to leave,
he realizes he is no longer perched
on the branch above the bar, but within the bar.
That is when he shouts *Fergit it*
fergit it. I'm gonna get drunk,
even though he's been hitting
the Oly since noon.

The Parrots of Easton do not forget.
The bar named Gladys does not forget.
And Wilby, the solitary Parrot
in his ironed-flat everything,
he can't forget either as he drinks
away the day, so that maybe this time
he can rise above the night.

Blackstone Avenue

You wanted to move through life
that way, on roller skates,
to matter the way lightning matters,
the way the woman on the poster,
all lips and sequins, matters,
to matter like an explosion
of imitation stars in the sky
on the darkest night in July.

When you roller skate
down Blackstone Avenue,
past all the yields,
past all the stop signs,
sooner or later, you smack
into something, like a billboard maybe,
and all that's left is the shape
of that cartoon creature,
arms outstretched,
a cutout, an outline of self.

Where do you start to fill it in?
How do you collect features
and face? You start, I think,
by slowing down, by listening,
even if you can't do more
than place your ear
against the asphalt.
In time, you will be able to find
your legs again, and although
at first, they may feel
more like water than like flesh,
they will carry you.

Judith Shakespeare Goes Postal

You have outlived Virginia Woolf
and her predictions, working under cover
at the Postal Annex, solving
the mysteries of Priority
and Express, charging by the ounce.
Today, you suggest the proper size
for a box of books being shipped
to a bald man's cousin in Iowa.

As I wait in line, I imagine you
upstairs, in an apartment of your own,
across the street from this strip mall,
writing at a white kitchen table,
your open window overlooking
the dusty orchards that border Highway 99.

If I asked you how you moved from
rumored suicide to the anonymity
of silence, you would probably tell me
that you did it the way most women do,
quietly, when no one was looking.

Then I would tell you that much has changed,
since your creation, except us,
our judgment of ourselves
and our willingness to bend,
always bend, when perhaps we should
just kick those brown cardboard boxes
against the wall, leave the key in
the cash register of the ruling,
turn the sign to Closed/*Cerrado,*
and get the hell out.

The books are packed, the bald man gone.
You ask how you may help me,
and I hear the telling melody in your voice
just before you hide it with a smile,
a lowering of tone.
But I know who you are, Judith,
and in the reflection of your face, I see it all.

You Imagine

In your backyard, the moonlight
illuminates an arm along the garden chair.
He is wearing a white shirt,
and something about his manner
makes you think of a boy
on his way to a school dance.
You imagine an accident
late at night and try not to think about
what happened to the other side of his face.

You feel him again
as the evenings chill with fall.
Over those weeks,
you cannot look outside
when the blinds are open.
You cannot even glance.

One night you stand at the window
and say, "If you have nothing for me,
and I have nothing for you,
then you must leave."
He does not return,
and you face the cold alone,
wondering why you were chosen,
or if you were the one
doing the choosing.

Then you remember the shot
you heard right after you moved here,
when everything about
the neighborhood was significant
and new.

In dreams, you connect
that shot and the boy,
trying to make sense of what brought
his shape to your patio,
and how he knew not to turn
to let you see the other side.

The Way They Leave

There they stand, wrapped in the long hair
of our youth, opening their arms
to the future. That girl, her bursting smile,
gone, wiped out by a car on a one-way street
while she tried to leave one more faithless lover.

The only poet who didn't drink, didn't smoke,
didn't cheat, sacrificed to cancer.
The one who rose every morning
with the Gallo Brothers in his coffee cup
sneaks into the poet's hospital room to chant,
drunk enough to think he can,
if not raise the dead, hang onto the living.

When the Brothers and their burgundy
catch up to him, and his ashes rain down
from a crop duster over his uncle's farm
in Reedley, we run like hell from
the funneling cloud.

There ought to be rules
as to the way the young depart
and the order in which they do.
The child would be rescued. The plane
would miss the towers. A sobbing woman
riding her bike down Van Ness Boulevard
would see the stop sign years before it appears.

By the very nature of our existence,
we play Russian Roulette without the gun,
watching the players dwindle,
knowing there is no winning number,
as the girl, the poet, the drunk look back at us,
and smile for the camera.

All The Time

You've seen him,
that boy,
his weekend smile
as he crosses the CVS parking lot
next to the apartment complex,
shiny dark hair below his ears,
pale arms at his side,
his friend shorter,
rounder, browner,
Afro lit gold by the sun.
They will cross the street
as they do every Saturday,
heading for the shopping center
with money and laughter to spend
and all the time in the world.

He will cross that parking lot,
that street, hundreds of times
before the future comes looking
for him, before the apartment
turns to dust and memory,
before he can no longer tolerate
the heat of the San Joaquin Valley
closing around him, naming him,
framing him, pointing out
how thin his arms, his dreams are.

This is a boy crossing a
parking lot, facing the traffic
of Milburn Avenue
and everything beyond,
not in a hurry, not today.

Momentary Women

Against smoke-filled skies
like a hazy memory
a white cloud presses.

We don't own
our bodies or our breaths.
And if we did, what then?
More? Less?

Eating the Poems

It is my latest diet. I eat my poems.
I am through with them, those flat,
black sentences that lie like boards
on a porch.

If I could pry them high enough,
I might find you underneath.
But I don't. I eat them,
tasteless, bland cottage-cheese poems.

Tonight, they will lie on my stomach,
weightless and white, like a man,
or the ghost of one.

Napa Valley Diptych

Bring together these elements that might
mix, might not.
Chug down thimbles of red,
swishes of white,
test tubes of bubbling sparklers.
Combine
and watch the results
from a safe distance,
just in case.

Take the smiling people
at Safeway,
their fluffed, pink cheeks.
Mix them with tourists.
You can always tell the tourists,
holding hands for balance,
for unity, for the good,
clean fun of it,
buying lambchops the price
of diamonds,
while, off the road,
growers spray sunscreen
on their grapes and
irrigate their vineyards
with treated wastewater.

If the experiment fails,
if the green hills wither to chaff,
if smoke marinates
the cabernet grapes
beyond recognition,
if the reservoir can no longer
give and give and give
then
sell those lambchops,
fill those test tubes,
and get everybody drunk by five.

Sequoia
    Containment

It is a teeter totter
42,000 acres so far
sparked in the park
by lightening
by light carriers
and light throwers
           Sequoia
Containment
1700 fire
fighters
air operations
ground crews
Sequoia
      Containment
Tule reservation
ancient ash of sequoias
devouring vegetation
              Sequoia
              wildfire
0% containment,
shooting
for the sky

Bat, Butterfly, Moth

A Rorschach cloud
hovers in a sky
of manganese blue.

It follows you home,
a shape you can't outrun,
the size of the state,
the state of the land.

It is the way here
in this valley of extremes.
You look for answers above,
trying to distinguish
the wildfire smoke
from the rain clouds,
seeking meaning
and maybe your own face
in that soft, smudged space
you almost recognize,
almost understand.

Bat, butterfly, moth
a memory,
a reminder,
a regret.

You see it in your sleep,
where it spreads like a storm,
like darkness spreads, like ink.

October Abstract

After the fires of
the San Joaquin,
you live and breathe
at the bottom of
a deep bowl of smoke,
the forgotten
California.

Then, in your sleep,
something shifts.
It starts as part of a dream,
intrusive and momentary
as hope.

At first, still lost in
the parched reality of waking,
you barely recognize
the soft brushstrokes
you now realize are drops
and the rhythm you recognize
as life.

Finally, the sooty sky
opens, and the rain falls.

With Thanks

Michelle Bogan
Annie Brantingham
John Brantingham
Dr. Elizabeth Carson-Murphy
Carrie Lynn Hawthorne
Larry Hill
Dr. Angel L. Martinez
Anette Nilsson
Dr. Nathan Singer
Jenny Toste

Antioch University Los Angeles MFA Program
Culturama, Mt. San Antonio College
The William Saroyan Society, Fresno, which will receive all author proceeds from this collection.

Critique group love: Hazel Dixon-Cooper and Stacy Renee Lucas

Bonnie Hearn Hill is the author of sixteen novels and four nonfiction books. Her poems have placed first in competitions including the Unitarian Universalist Awards, Chabot College Awards, and California State Poetry Society Awards, and her articles on writing have appeared in *Publishers Weekly, The Writer, Writer's Digest*, and other publications.

www.bonniehhill.com

www.ingramcontent.com/pod-product-compliance
Lightning Source LLC
Chambersburg PA
CBHW022128090426
42743CB00008B/1061